W9-AWX-188

Totally Strange Buildings

by Lisa M. Herrington

Content Consultant

Robbin Friedman, Children's Librarian
Chappaqua (N.Y.) Library

Reading Consultant

Jeanne M. Clidas, Ph.D.
Reading Specialistt

Children's Press®
An Imprint of Scholastic Inc.

Library of Congress Cataloging-in-Publication Data

Names: Herrington, Lisa M.
Title: Totally strange buildings/by Lisa M. Herrington.
Description: New York, NY: Children's Press, [2017] | Series: Rookie amazing America | Includes index.
Identifiers: LCCN 2016030321 | ISBN 9780531228975 (library binding) | ISBN 9780531225912 (pbk.)
Subjects: LCSH: Buildings—Miscellanea—Juvenile literature. | Structural engineering—Juvenile literature.
Classification: LCC TH149 .H47 2017 | DDC 690—dc23
LC record available at https://lccn.loc.gov/2016030321

No part of this publication may be reproduced in whole or in part, or stored in a retrieval system, or transmitted in any form or by any means, electronic, mechanical, photocopying, recording, or otherwise, without written permission of the publisher. For information regarding permission, write to Scholastic Inc., Attention: Permissions Department, 557 Broadway, New York, NY 10012.

Produced by Spooky Cheetah Press

© 2017 by Scholastic Inc.

All rights reserved. Published in 2017 by Children's Press, an imprint of Scholastic Inc.

Printed in China 62

SCHOLASTIC, CHILDREN'S PRESS, ROOKIE AMAZING AMERICA™, and associated logos are trademarks and/or registered trademarks of Scholastic Inc.

1 2 3 4 5 6 7 8 9 10 R 26 25 24 23 22 21 20 19 18 17

Photographs ©: cover: Douglas Keister; back cover: Design Pics Inc/Alamy Images; 3: TinaImages/Shutterstock, Inc.; 4: MGH/Shutterstock, Inc.; 5: Christina Lundeen/Getty Images; 6: 3DSculptor/iStockphoto; 7 main: Stefano Politi Markovina/Getty Images; 7 inset: View Pictures/UIG/Getty Images; 8-9 main: Arina P Habich/Shutterstock, Inc.; 9 left inset: Scott Prokop/Shutterstock, Inc.; 9 right inset: Jeffrey Kaphan/Getty Images; 10-11: Clarence Martin/Dreamstime; 12: Geoff Kuchera/iStockphoto; 13: tusharkoley/Shutterstock, Inc.; 14 right inset: Brett Beyer/Getty Images; 14 left inset: Lucas Jackson/EPA/Newscom; 14-15 main: f11photo/Shutterstock, Inc.; 16-17: Allard Schager/Getty Images; 18-19: Ricardo DeAratanha/Los Angeles Times/Getty Images; 20-21: UrbanTexture/Alamy Images; 22-23: Douglas Keister; 24 inset: Education Images/UIG/Getty Images; 24-25 main: Design Pics Inc/Alamy Images; 26-27 background: 123ducu/iStockphoto; 26 top left: tusharkoley/Shutterstock, Inc.; 26 top center: f11photo/Shutterstock, Inc.; 26 top right: Ricardo DeAratanha/Los Angeles Times/Getty Images; 26 center left: Douglas Keister; 26 center: Stefano Politi Markovina/Getty Images; 26 center right: Design Pics Inc/Alamy Images; 26 bottom left: MGH/Shutterstock, Inc.; 26 bottom center: UrbanTexture/Alamy Images; 26 bottom right: Arina P Habich/Shutterstock, Inc.; 28-29 background: ooyoo/iStockphoto; 28 main: Wim Wiskerke/Alamy Images; 29 main: Nataliya Hora/Dreamstime; 30 main: alexsvirid/Shutterstock, Inc.; 30 background: 123ducu/iStockphoto; 31 top: PeopleImages/iStockphoto; 31 bottom: Allard Schager/Getty Images; 31 center bottom: MGH/Shutterstock, Inc.; 31 center top: f11photo/Shutterstock, Inc.; 32: Douglas Keister.

Maps by Jim McMahon.

Table of Contents

Introduction 4

What Does It Look Like? 6

Skyscraper Superstars 12

From Stone to Steel 18

Strange Houses and Museums 22

Map Quest 26

Which Is More Amazing? You Decide! 28

You Name It 30

Glossary 31

Index 32

Facts for Now 32

About the Author 32

Introduction

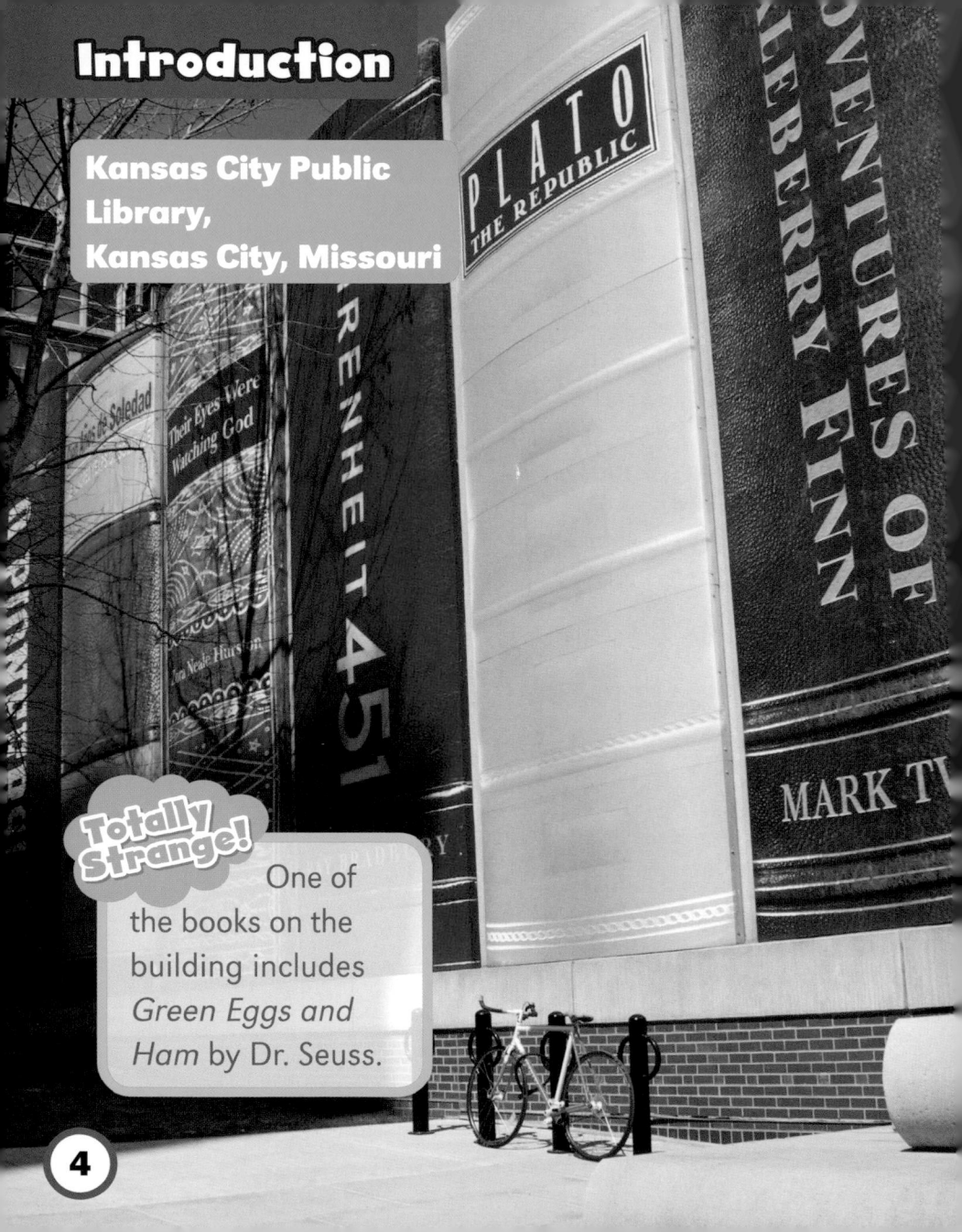

Kansas City Public Library, Kansas City, Missouri

Totally Strange!

One of the books on the building includes *Green Eggs and Ham* by Dr. Seuss.

Is that a shelf from the world's biggest bookstore?

No! It is the Kansas City Public Library. The walls of the parking garage look like giant book **spines**.

There are lots of amazing buildings across the United States. This library is just one of them. Let's explore more!

What Does It Look Like?

This building looks like a ship. It is the Walt Disney Concert Hall. Music concerts are held here.

The **architect** who designed the concert hall loves the sea. Do you think this building's curves look like the sails on a ship?

ship

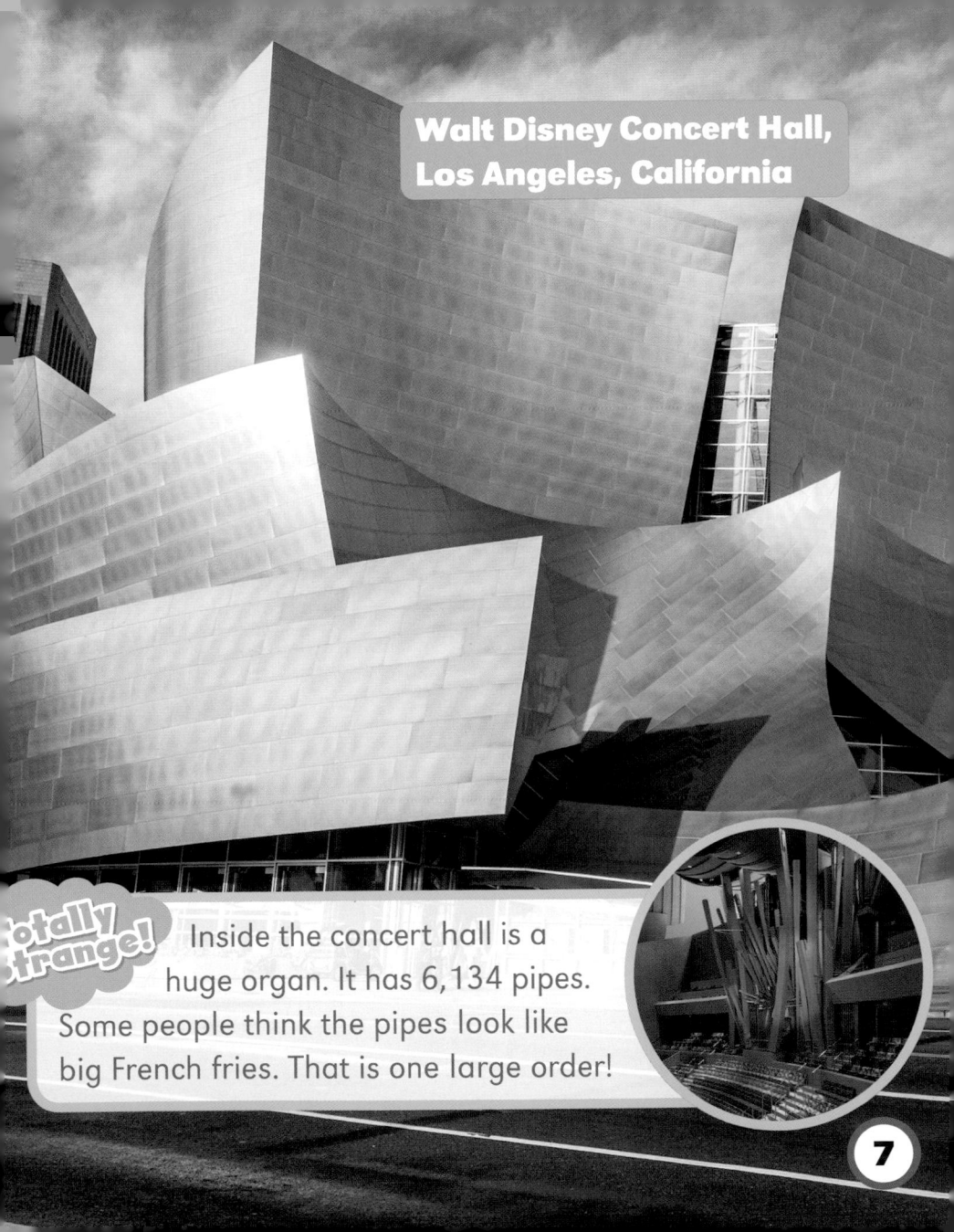

Walt Disney Concert Hall, Los Angeles, California

Totally Strange! Inside the concert hall is a huge organ. It has 6,134 pipes. Some people think the pipes look like big French fries. That is one large order!

Can you guess what this building is used for? It is an airport. Its roof is made of fabric triangles.

It was designed to match the shape of the nearby mountains.

Denver International Airport, Denver, Colorado

The triangles also look like American Indian teepees that were found nearby long ago.

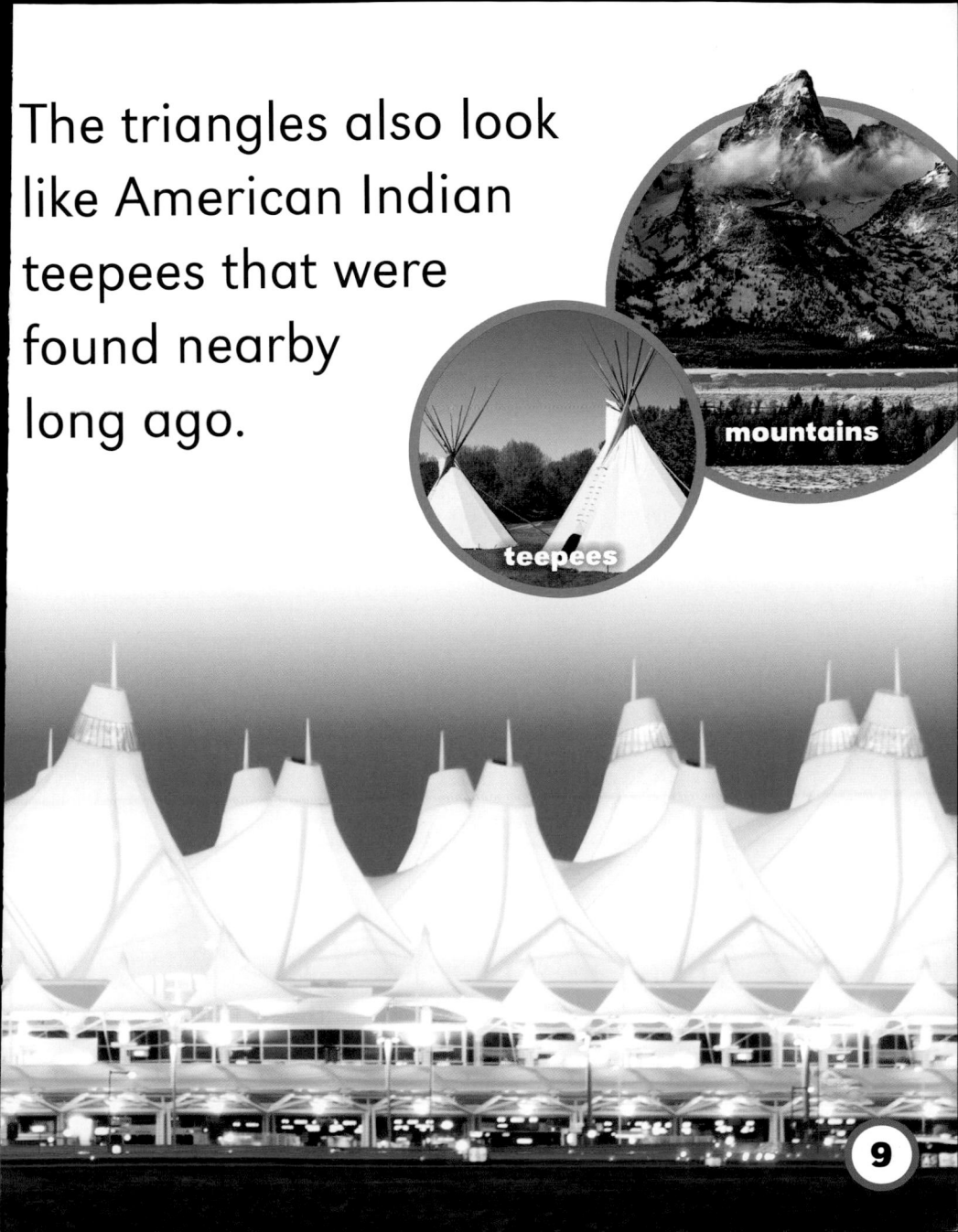

This building might make you think of picnics. It looks like the world's biggest basket! It used to be home to a basket-making company.

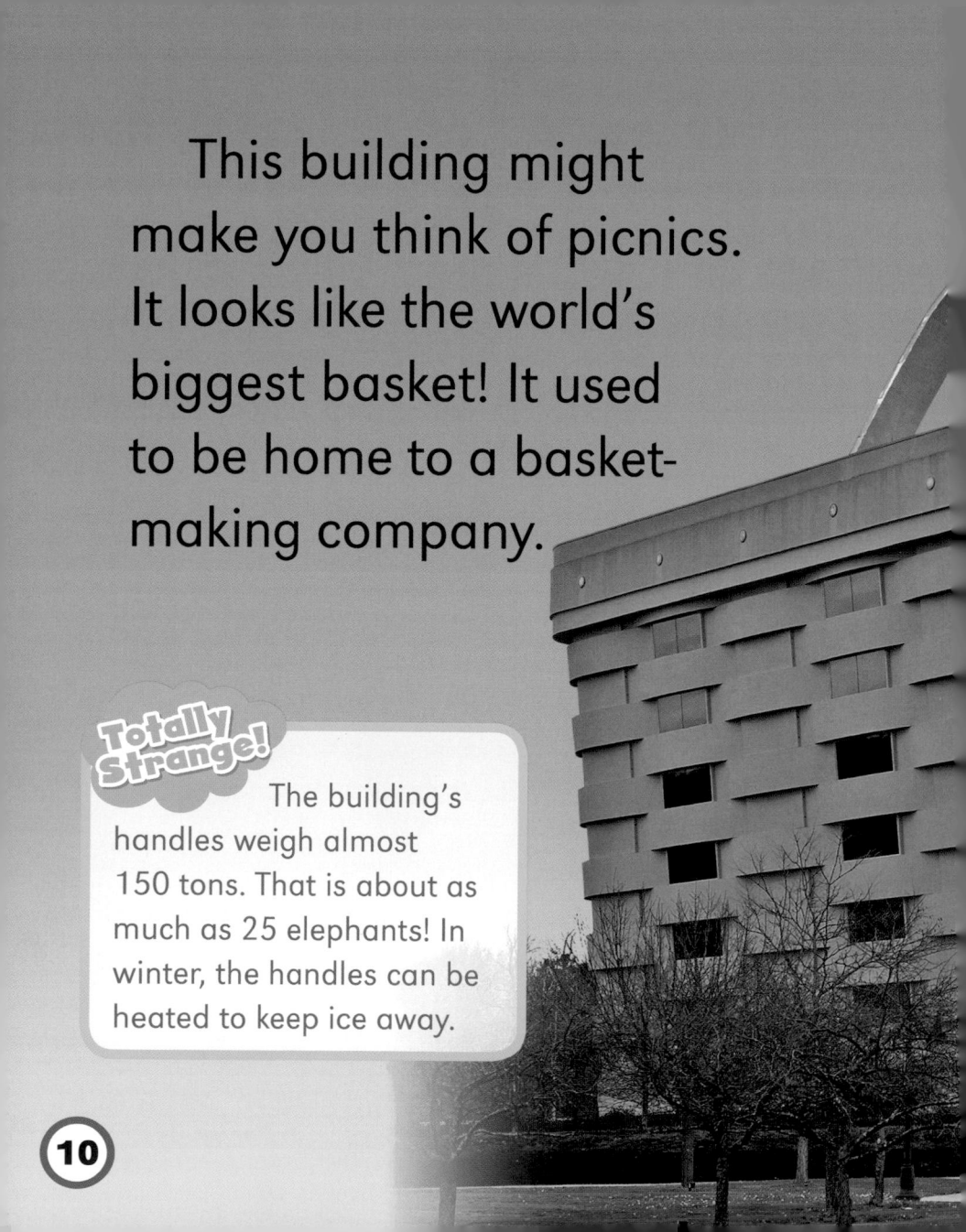

Totally Strange!

The building's handles weigh almost 150 tons. That is about as much as 25 elephants! In winter, the handles can be heated to keep ice away.

Basket Building, Newark, Ohio

Skyscraper Superstars

The tallest buildings are known as **skyscrapers**. This one looks like a flying saucer! It is the Space Needle. It is 605 feet (184 meters) high. That is about as tall as 30 giraffes!

The Space Needle has an hourglass shape. A restaurant on top gives visitors a view of Seattle.

Space Needle, Seattle, Washington

Totally Strange!

The Space Needle was built in just 400 days.

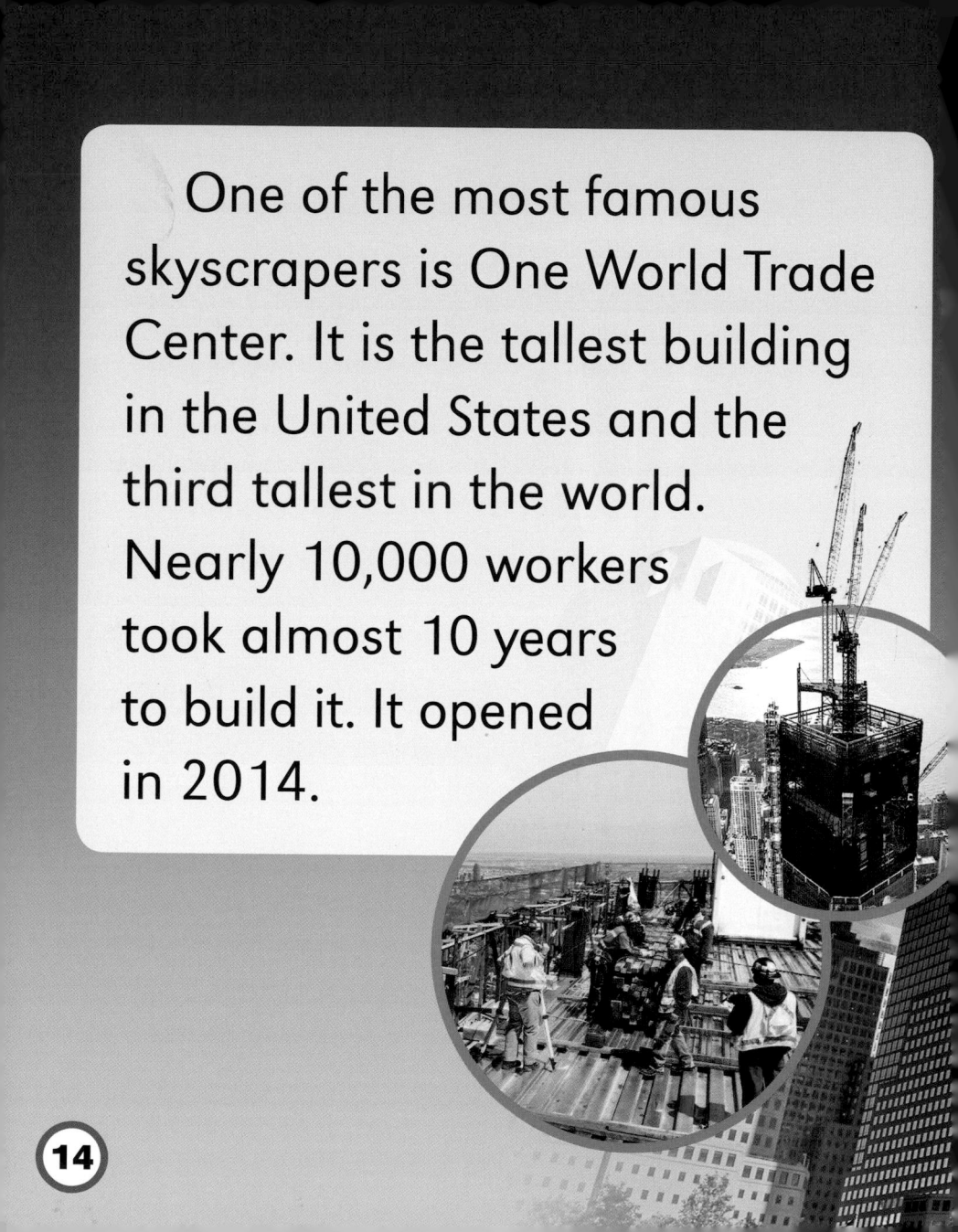

One of the most famous skyscrapers is One World Trade Center. It is the tallest building in the United States and the third tallest in the world. Nearly 10,000 workers took almost 10 years to build it. It opened in 2014.

One World Trade Center, New York, New York

This building looks like it is twisting as it rises.

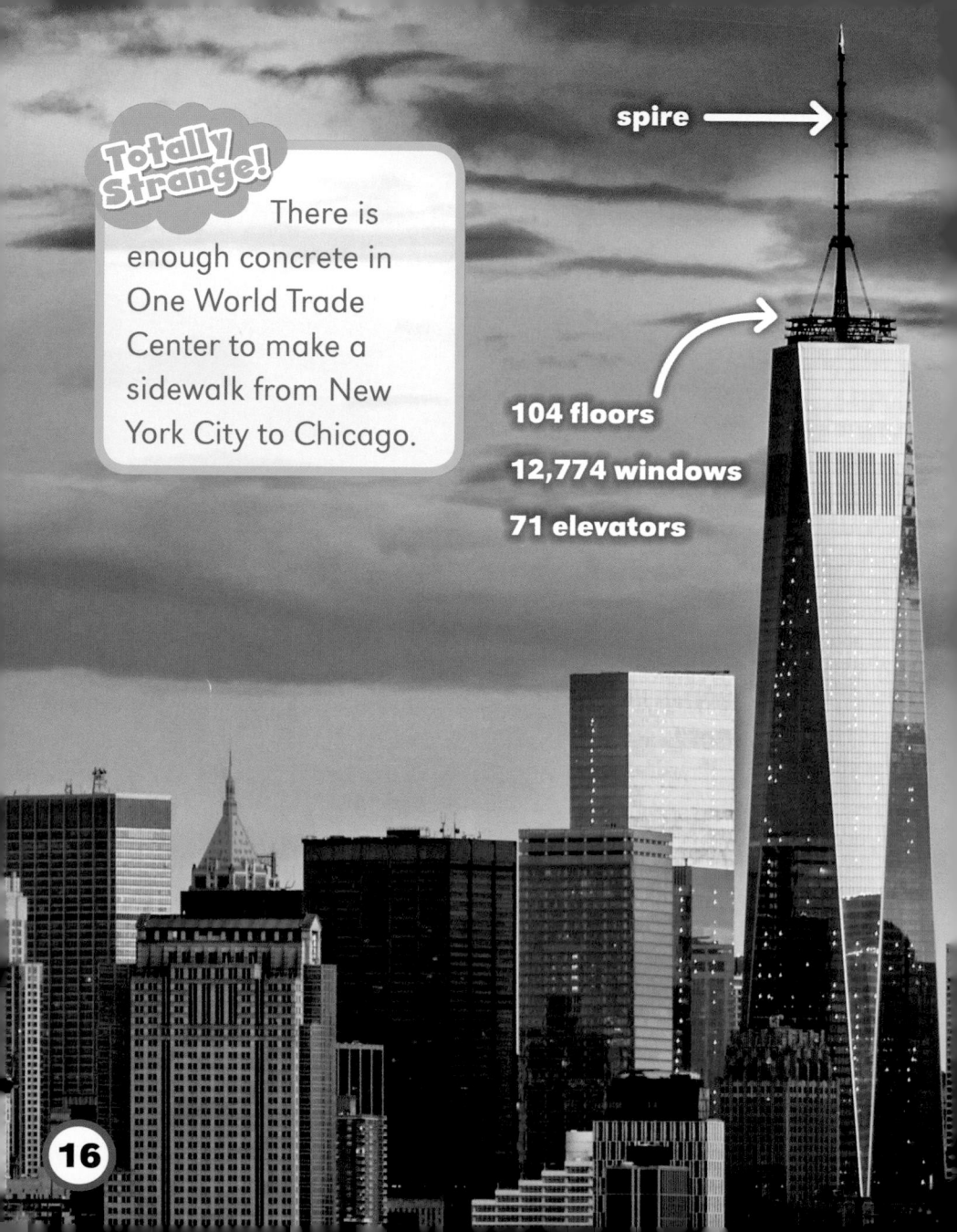

Totally Strange!

There is enough concrete in One World Trade Center to make a sidewalk from New York City to Chicago.

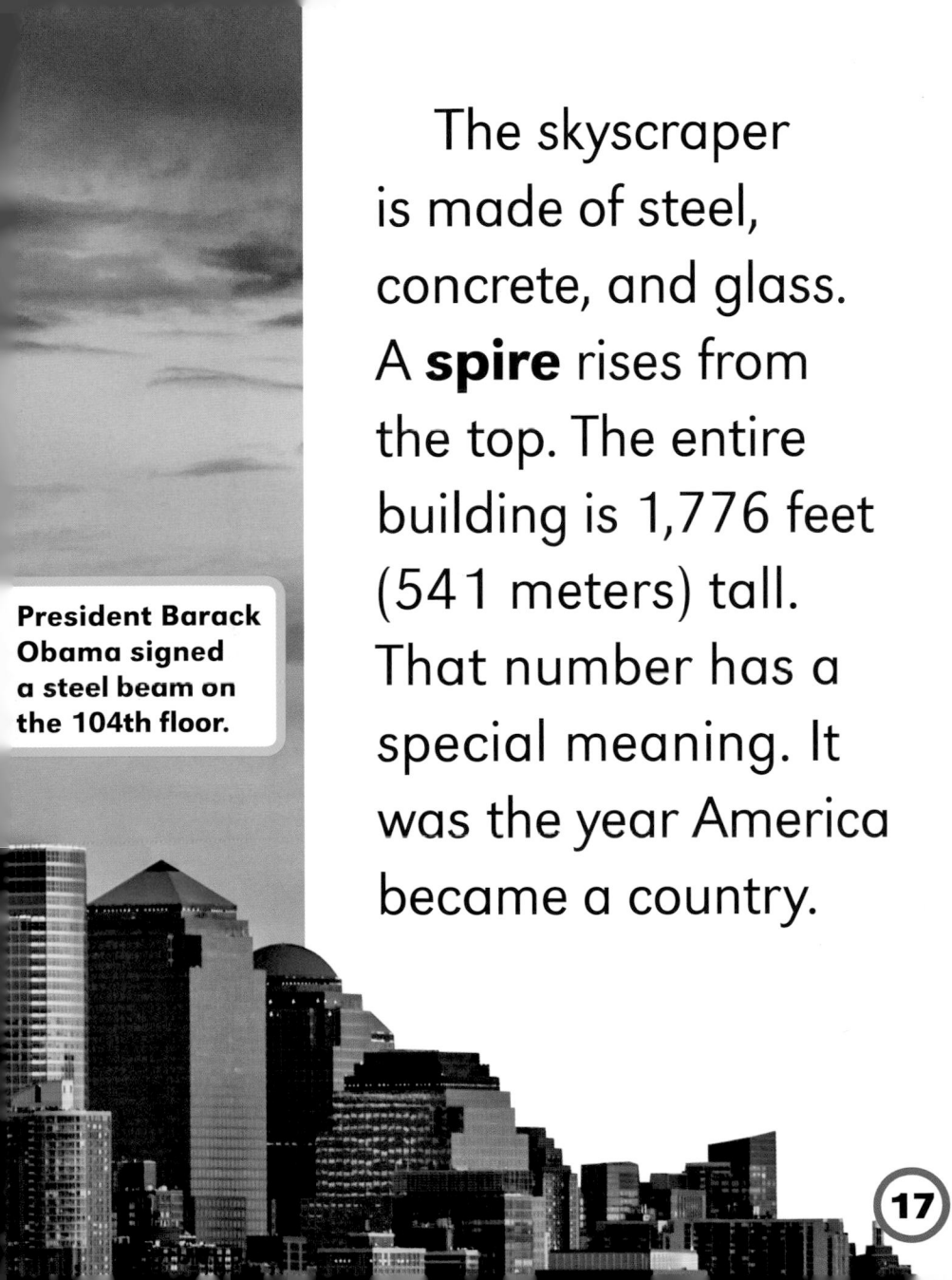

President Barack Obama signed a steel beam on the 104th floor.

The skyscraper is made of steel, concrete, and glass. A **spire** rises from the top. The entire building is 1,776 feet (541 meters) tall. That number has a special meaning. It was the year America became a country.

From Stone to Steel

Some buildings are in surprising places. This chapel is built into the red rocks of Arizona.

The Chapel of the Holy Cross stands on top of a hill. The spot was chosen for its peaceful views.

Chapel of the Holy Cross, Sedona, Arizona

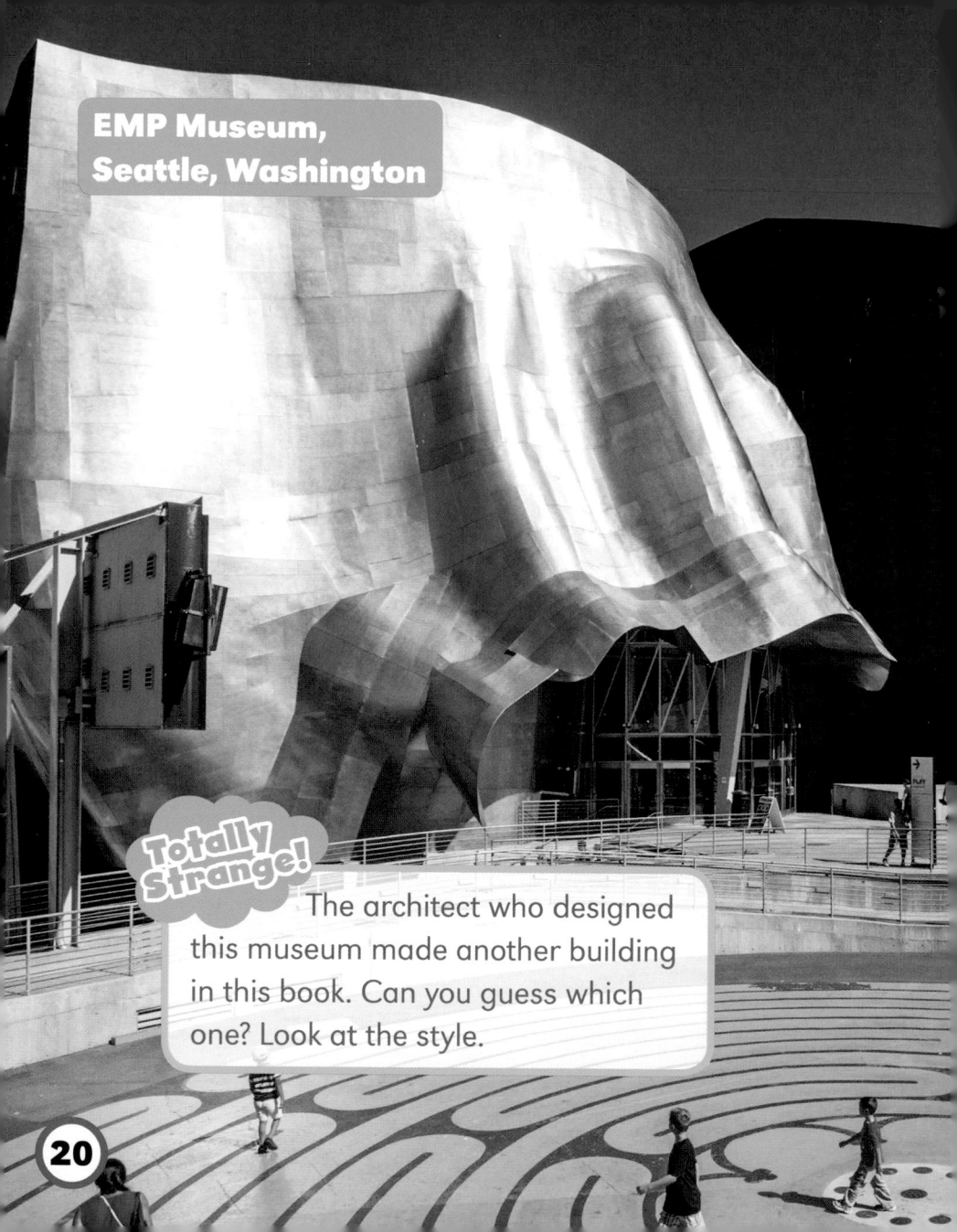

EMP Museum, Seattle, Washington

Totally Strange!

The architect who designed this museum made another building in this book. Can you guess which one? Look at the style.

What a wild building! Visitors come to the EMP Museum to learn about music, movies, and more. The building is made from more than 21,000 metal pieces. Its curvy design is meant to show movement and energy.

Answer: Both the EMP Museum and the Walt Disney Concert Hall were designed by Frank Gehry.

Strange Houses and Museums

Once upon a time...someone built a storybook house. This house looks like it is from a fairy tale.

Storybook houses like this one are made to be fun and playful. Snow White and the Seven Dwarfs could live here!

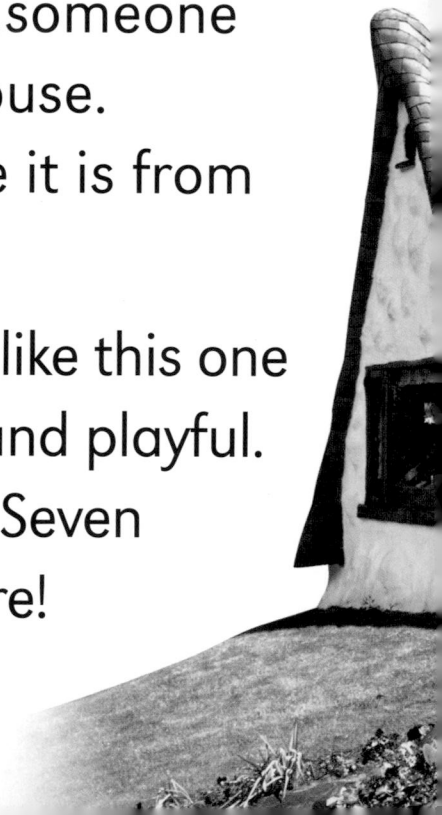

Storybook House, Olalla, Washington
What makes a storybook house?
pointy, uneven roof
odd-shaped doors and windows
stone walkway

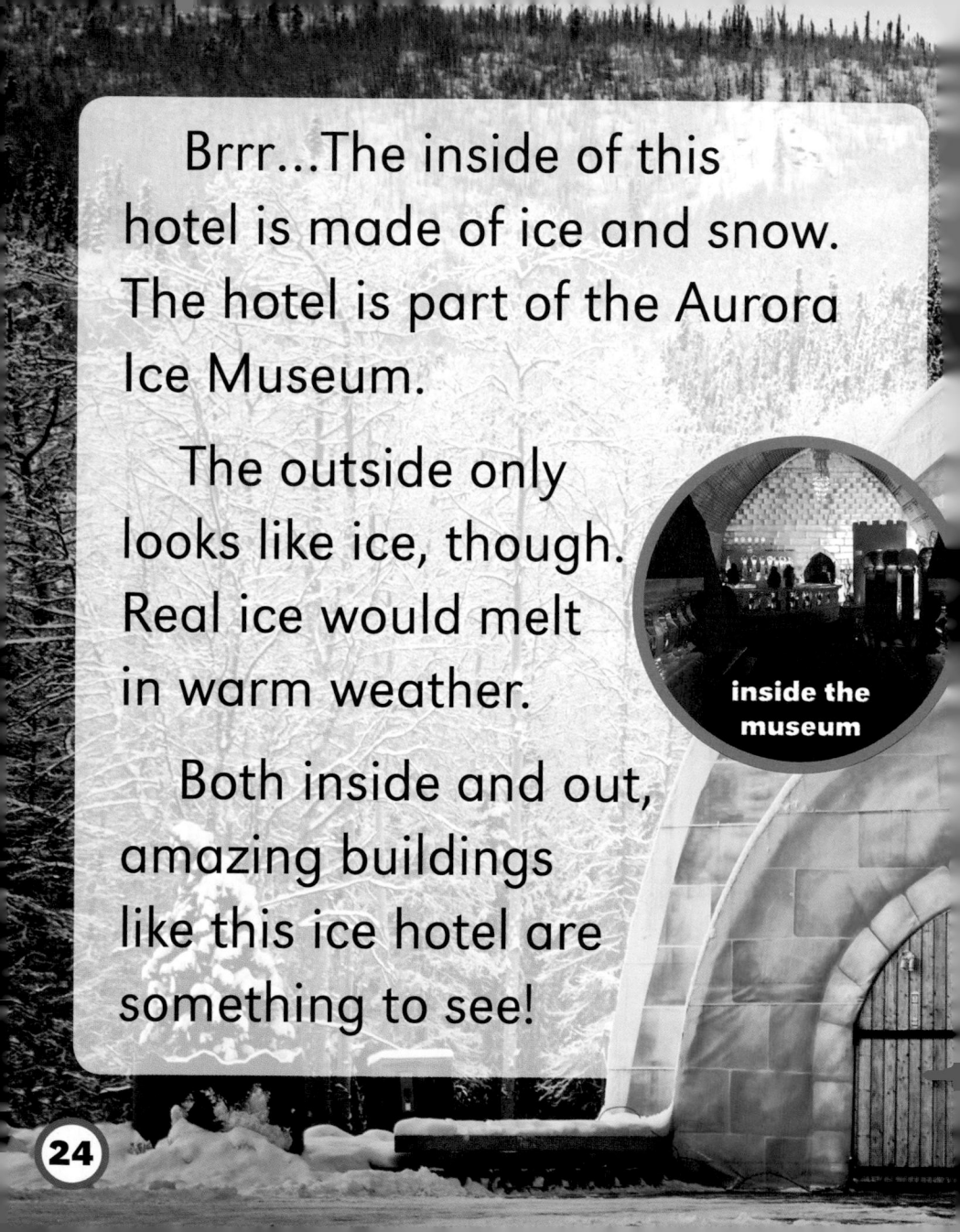

Brrr...The inside of this hotel is made of ice and snow. The hotel is part of the Aurora Ice Museum.

The outside only looks like ice, though. Real ice would melt in warm weather.

Both inside and out, amazing buildings like this ice hotel are something to see!

inside the museum

Aurora Ice Museum, Fairbanks, Alaska

United States

Can you find each of our totally strange buildings on the map below?

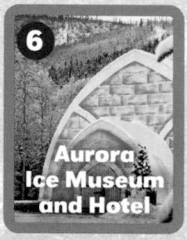

Alaska and Hawaii are not drawn to scale or placed in their proper place

# of America

New Hampshire
Maine
Michigan
Vermont
Minnesota
North Dakota
Massachusetts
New York
Wisconsin
South Dakota
Rhode Island
2
Connecticut
Pennsylvania
ming
New Jersey
Iowa
Ohio
Nebraska
Illinois
Delaware
Indiana
West Virginia
Maryland
9
7
Virginia
Washington, D.C.
(U.S. capital)
orado
Kansas
Missouri
Kentucky
North Carolina
Tennessee
South Carolina
Oklahoma
Arkansas
Alabama
xico
Georgia
Texas
Louisiana
Florida
Mississippi
Compass Rose
North
West
East
South

Which Is More

Haines Shoe House, Hellam, Pennsylvania

- A couple lives in this shoe house. The living room is in the toe. The kitchen is in the heel.
- A shoe salesman had the house made. It was created to look like a work boot.
- The house sits on Shoe House Road. It is open for tours and ice cream.

Strange? You Decide!

WonderWorks, Orlando, Florida

- This wacky, upside-down building is an amusement park.
- Inside the building there are hurricane and earthquake rides.
- This building was designed to look like it was carried by a tornado and dropped on the side of a street.

You Name It

This building's design is a slam dunk! Can you guess which sport it honors?

Hint: *A gym teacher invented the sport in 1891. His students had to throw a ball into peach baskets.*

Answer: Basketball. The building is the Naismith Memorial Basketball Hall of Fame in Springfield, Massachusetts.

Glossary

- **architect** (AHR-kih-tekt): person who designs buildings and supervises the way they are built

- **skyscrapers** (SKY-skray-purz): very tall buildings

- **spines** (SPINES): on book covers, the part to which the pages are attached

- **spire** (SPIRE): structure that comes to a point at the top

Index

architect 6, 20

Aurora Ice Museum 24–25

Basket Building 10–11

Chapel of the Holy Cross 18–19

Denver International Airport 8–9

EMP Museum 20–21

Kansas City Public Library 5

Obama, President Barack 17

One World Trade Center 14–17

Space Needle 12–13

Storybook House 22–23

Walt Disney Concert Hall 6–7

Facts for Now

Visit this Scholastic Web site for more information on Strange Buildings:

www.factsfornow.scholastic.com

Enter the keywords Strange Buildings

About the Author

Lisa M. Herrington loves to write for children. She lives in a not-so-unusual house in Trumbull, Connecticut, with her husband and daughter.